A Little
Book of
Succulents

Running Press
Hachette Book Group
1290 Avenue of the Americas, New York, NY 10104
www.runningpress.com
@Running_Press

First Edition: April 2018

Published by Running Press, an imprint of Perseus Books, LLC, a subsidiary of Hachette Book Group, Inc.

The Hachette Speakers Bureau provides a wide range of authors for speaking events. To find out more, go to www.hachettespeakersbureau.com or call (866) 376-6591.

The publisher is not responsible for websites (or their content) that are not owned by the publisher.

ISBN: 978-0-7624-6371-8

Introduction

Succulents are adorable. They are tiny and sweet, and their little spikes and thorns feel like the claws of a kitten—sharp, but part of their charm.

The only problem is, succulents are not quite as easy to care for as one might assume. You would think that plants that thrive in low-water environments wouldn't be particularly finicky, but if they

aren't in that specific setting—
if they are, instead, in your office or
your house—succulents can be as
troublesome as any other plant, or
even more so. They require a lot of
direct sunlight, but not too much
heat, and certainly not too much
cold. Enough water, but not too
much, and on and on.

Felt succulents require no
fuss whatsoever, and they are just
as fun, creative, and adorable as
the living version—and they're
spike-free.

You'll need a pair of scissors for this project, but everything else is included!

Instructions

These instructions are for a multi-colored succulent, but feel free to make yours a solid color by using both felt sheets in the same shade.

1. Cut out 4 of the larger cross-shaped pieces of felt, 2 in each color. If you want, you can trim the rounded edges to make the leaves more pointed.

2. Cut out 2 of the smaller cross-shaped pieces, 1 in each color.

Again, trim the edges to make pointy leaves, if desired.

3. Decide which color you want to have on top, or if you want to alternate. These instructions are for purple on top of green.

4. Place one larger purple cross on top of a large green cross, and repeat with the other two large crosses. Lay them crosswise, so that eight leaves are showing.

5. Place the smaller purple cross on top of the smaller green cross, and lay them crosswise on top of the larger crosses.

6. Insert the straight pin into the center of the smaller crosses, pinning all the leaves in place, or use a needle and thread to secure your succulent.

7. Set your succulent in your pot and enjoy! You can always un-pin it and rearrange the petals whenever you want a new look.

Succulent
SPOTLIGHTS

Echeveria

Also known as the Desert Rose, Echevaria is a rosette-style succulent, but one that grows in a variety of colors. It can be pink, a dusky purple, orange, red, blue, or green with red tips. Echeveria can be pointed or rounded, and requires sandy soil with good drainage and fairly consistent temperatures—unless it is made of felt, as yours is.

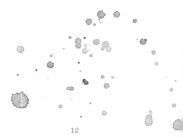

Hens &
Chicks

Hens and Chicks are one of the many rosette-style succulents, like the one featured in this kit, but they are so-called because of their tendency to produce *a lot* of babies.

Unlike many succulents, they are alpine plants, so they can tolerate cool weather as well as low water. They thrive where they have lots of room to propagate; the mother will die off after about six years, and chicks should be separated from their siblings to avoid overcrowding.

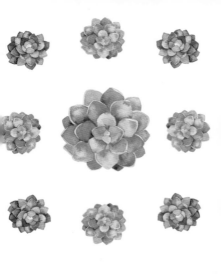

String
of Pearls

String of Pearls is a succulent
vine, which is fairly unusual,
and it looks just as it sounds—
though the pearls are quite
large, and have a bit of a
point on them, much like an

oyster that held onto its green
pearl as it was pulled out.
In its natural environment,
String of Pearls grows along
the earth, but it is commonly
grown in a hanging basket,
where it can trail seven
or eight feet down to the
ground. It produces small
white flowers that smell like
cinnamon.

Christmas Cactus

The Latin name of Christmas Cactus is *Schlumbergera,* so it's understandable why it was renamed something more festive. This succulent has no leaves; its green, fleshy stems perform all the required photosynthesis to keep the plant alive. The stems grow in segments, each with different facets, like a folded piece of paper. It blooms often, with elongated pink flowers.

Panda Plant

Unsurprisingly, Panda Plants (also known as Pussy Ears) are a favorite of children. They are small, fuzzy succulents, and their light green leaves are tipped with a deep brownish red, much the same color as a red panda. In their native environment, these plants can grow to be about the size of a panda, but indoor growth is limited by the size of the container.

Pincushion Cactus

Less beloved by children, the pincushion cactus can be fairly painful! A pincushion cactus is pretty much exactly what it sounds like—a fuzzy round ball with sharp points sticking out of it. It produces small flowers that grow like a crown around the top of the cactus, and the flowers can be either yellow, bright pink, or red.